Raising Good Tweens of Value:

The Ultimate Strategies for Unlocking Your Tween's Full Potential.

By

Charles T. Ellison

Table of contents

Introduction

In a world overflowing with limitless diversions and ever-evolving problems, the struggle to raise kids who exemplify integrity, compassion, and a strong sense of purpose has never been more vital. "Raising Good Tweens of Value," a deep book by the acclaimed author Charles T. Ellison, emerges as a guiding beacon in the chaotic sea of parenting throughout the tween years. With a combination of knowledge, competence, and profound empathy, Ellison's book offers a thorough guide for parents and caregivers, helping them to negotiate the transitional time between childhood and adolescence with grace and purpose. In "Raising Good Tweens of Value," Charles T. Ellison examines the varied process of fostering tweens who are not just excellent but great individuals who will go on to lead, inspire, and make a lasting effect on the world. Drawing on his depth of experience in child psychology and family dynamics, Ellison presents a fascinating tale rich with personal anecdotes, practical guidance, and deep insights. This book exceeds the typical scope of parenting manuals. It goes deep into the complexity of character development, resiliency, and moral growth, addressing the specific problems adolescents experience in a digital world. Ellison's knowledge shows as he navigates subjects such as peer pressure, screen time management, and building a sense of responsibility in tweens.

"Raising Good Tweens of Value" is more than a book; it is a beacon of hope for parents attempting to inculcate values, empathy, and leadership in their children. Ellison's remarks reverberate as a call to action for families striving to build a better future by growing adolescents who are not only successful but also sensitive, morally grounded, and motivated to make a difference. This book is a must-read for anyone involved in the future of our youth. With its engaging style, real-world examples, and accessible techniques, "Raising Good Tweens of Value" provides a lifeline to parents and caregivers, helping them on a transforming path towards creating tweens of outstanding value.

Chapter 1

What is tween?

Understanding the tweens stages

What is tween?

Tween is a word often used to refer to preadolescent or early adolescent individuals, typically between the ages of 9 and 12. It's a transitional stage of development between childhood and adolescence, hence the name "tween," which is an abbreviation of "between." Tweens are often characterized by their emerging independence, the formation of personal interests, and the discovery of their identities. This term is extensively used in marketing and media to target this specific age group with products and information geared to their interests and needs.

Understanding the tweens stages

The tween period, usually referred to as preadolescence, is a major transitional period in human development that generally occurs between the ages of 9 and 12. This age spans the bridge between childhood and adolescence and is defined by profound physical, cognitive, and emotional changes.

Physically

tweens undergo quick growth spurts, with the onset of puberty becoming more obvious. Hormonal changes lead to the development of secondary sexual features, such as breast development in females and facial hair growth in boys.

Cognitively

Ttweens demonstrate higher cognitive capacities, including more complicated problem-solving skills and a rising aptitude for abstract reasoning. They become increasingly independent in their decision-making and often start to form their own views and ideals.

Emotionally

Tweens may grapple with increased self-awareness, peer pressure, and a craving for greater autonomy. They may endure mood swings and seek to study their identities more deeply. Understanding the tween stage is crucial for parents, educators, and caregivers to provide appropriate support and guidance during this key period of development, ensuring that tweens manage these transitions successfully and emerge as confident adolescents.

Chapter 2

Parenting philosophy

Defining your parenting values

Creating a family mission statement

Parenting Philosophy

Parenting philosophy is the cornerstone upon which a parent's approach to raising children is constructed. It contains a set of beliefs, values, and principles that influence every element of the parenting process. Essentially, it is a guide for nurturing and developing the next generation. At its foundation, parenting philosophy helps parents comprehend and define their role in a child's life. It is a reflection of the parent's character, upbringing, and the hopes they have for their children. Every parent, consciously or subconsciously, follows a distinct parenting philosophy that shapes their choices, behaviors, and relationships with their children. Defining one's parenting philosophy is a critical stage in the path of motherhood. It requires assessing personal values, beliefs, and priorities. Are you a supporter of discipline or a proponent of free-spirited creativity? Do you prioritize independence or foster interdependence? These questions underlie your parenting philosophy and influence the sort of parent you become.

Furthermore, a well-considered parenting philosophy is not static but grows through time as parents learn and adjust to the changing needs of their children. It aids parents in creating limits, imparting morality, and building a caring and nurturing atmosphere. It works as a guiding star in instances of uncertainty or decision-making. Parenting philosophy is a cornerstone of successful and deliberate parenting.

It is the compass that helps parents navigate the trials and pleasures of parenting children. By establishing their parenting philosophy, parents may seek to provide a supportive, caring, and enriching environment for their children, helping them develop into confident and well-rounded people.

Defining your parenting values

Defining your parenting values is a vital step in developing well-rounded, responsible, and joyful children. These principles serve as the compass that guides your parenting journey, forming your children's character and affecting their future choices. First and foremost, self-reflection is vital. It's vital to examine your particular principles and views. What ideals do you hold dear? Whether it's honesty, empathy, respect, or persistence, recognizing your basic beliefs is the cornerstone of great parenting. Next, evaluate the larger socioeconomic background. Recognize the values and traits you wish to impart to your children. You may strive to produce socially responsible people who embrace variety and inclusiveness. Understanding the global community's values might help you modify your parenting strategy properly.

Consistency is crucial in parenting. Your ideals should be clearly articulated and constantly reinforced. This constancy gives youngsters a steady foundation to establish their own moral compass.

Adaptability is also vital.

Parenting principles may need to adapt to your child's development and changing circumstances. Staying open to fresh viewpoints and being ready to adapt your approach helps support healthy growth. Moreover, lead by example. Children typically replicate their parents' habits and attitudes. Demonstrating your principles through your own activities will create a lasting impact. Defining your parenting principles is a constant effort. It needs self-awareness, adaptation, and regular communication.

By doing so, you provide a loving atmosphere in which your children may learn, grow, and eventually establish their own values, putting them on a road to being responsible, ethical, and empathic adults.

Creating a family mission statement

A family mission statement is a strong and meaningful proclamation that specifies the values, aims, and principles that govern a family's collective journey through life. It functions as a compass, connecting family members with a single goal and generating a feeling of oneness. This contract often contains essential values, such as love, respect, and honesty, which family members vow to preserve. A well-crafted family mission statement emphasizes particular aims and desires, such as valuing quality time together, supporting one another's dreams, or giving to the community. It may also stress the necessity of open communication and dispute resolution. By explicitly defining these aims, a family purpose statement helps guarantee that all members are on the same page, producing a peaceful atmosphere. Besides, the act of establishing a family purpose statement may be a bonding event in itself. It stimulates serious talk and contemplation, enabling each family member to voice their beliefs and aspirations. Crafting and reviewing the statement frequently may strengthen the family's dedication to its objective and alter it as circumstances change.

Chapter 3

Listening and empathy

Open and honest conversations

Listening and empathy

Listening and empathy are two interrelated traits that play a crucial role in successful communication and developing lasting connections. Listening requires not simply hearing words but also comprehending their underlying feelings and intentions. It is an active and intentional procedure that requires one's complete attention. Empathy, on the other hand, is the capacity to put oneself in another person's shoes and comprehend their thoughts and viewpoints. When these two aspects come together, significant relationships are established. Empathetic listening fosters a secure atmosphere for open communication where people feel heard and valued. This, in turn, develops trust and understanding between individuals. In professional contexts, empathic listening may increase cooperation and problem-solving since it encourages greater collaboration and conflict resolution. Empathy and listening are also crucial in personal connections. When someone feels really heard and understood, their emotional well-being is strengthened, leading to greater ties. Additionally, empathy helps calm confrontations by respecting another's point of view. In a society defined by quick digital communication, these talents are frequently disregarded, although they remain vital for human connection. By deliberately mastering the skill of listening with empathy, people may traverse the intricacies of human relationships, creating peace and enhancing their personal and professional lives.

Open and honest dialogue

Open and honest dialogues are the core of good communication and strong relationships. Such talks contain the open interchange of ideas, sentiments, and facts without concealment or dishonesty. This openness develops trust, strengthens relationships, and enhances understanding between people and among communities. In intimate relationships, open and honest dialogues offer the basis for closeness and emotional development. They help partners communicate their wants, anxieties, and desires, resulting in improved problem-solving and conflict resolution. Furthermore, they provide an atmosphere where people may be their real selves, fostering self-acceptance and empathy. In the professional domain, open and honest communication is vital for cooperation, creativity, and ethical decision-making. Teams that enable open dialogue benefit from varied viewpoints, enabling innovative problem-solving and higher productivity. Transparent communication within firms creates trust, employee morale, and a culture of responsibility. Open and honest dialogue plays a crucial role in society's advancement. They inspire social change, create empathy, and bridge differences by permitting talks about challenging themes like race, politics, and inequality. Open and honest dialogues are not only vital for personal and professional relationships but are also crucial to developing a more equitable and peaceful society. Encouraging these talks allows people to speak their truth and builds a culture where honesty, understanding, and development may flourish. Navigating tough debates is a crucial ability in both personal and professional life. Such talks typically entail delicate themes, diverse perspectives, and strong emotions, making them potential minefields if not treated with caution. To manage these debates successfully, many fundamental concepts should be addressed.

First, active listening is crucial. Show empathy and genuine interest in the other person's viewpoint. Avoid interrupting or leaping to conclusions. Instead, use open-ended questions to explain and grasp their position better. Maintaining respect is another crucial issue. Even when differences develop, it's crucial to treat all parties with politeness and avoid personal attacks. Focus on the topic at hand, not the individual. Furthermore, maintaining a comfortable workplace fosters open communication.

Assure all participants that their voices will be heard without judgment. This might require creating ground rules for the debate, such as avoiding blaming or insulting words. In difficult debates, it's frequently beneficial to discover common ground and expand from there. Identify similar aims or beliefs to bridge gaps and work towards a solution. Lastly, knowing the power of compromise is vital. In many circumstances, a perfect settlement may not be feasible, but finding a middle ground may lead to growth and the retention of relationships. Navigating hard topics takes active listening, respect, providing a safe space, identifying common ground, and accepting compromise. By learning these concepts, people may handle tough conversations with grace, enabling understanding and resolution even in the face of hardship.

Chapter 4

Establishing house rules

Consistency in discipline

Teaching responsibility

Establishing house rules

Establishing home rules is vital for keeping a pleasant and well-functioning family. These standards serve as a blueprint for family members to navigate everyday life, emphasizing respect, order, and collaboration. House rules often encompass many elements of living together. First and foremost, they establish standards for conduct and duties. This includes regulations on tasks, mealtime manners, and curfews, which help reduce disputes and guarantee that everyone contributes to the household's care. Furthermore, home rules may address safety and privacy problems. For instance, regulations on securing doors, managing domestic appliances, and maintaining personal boundaries help create a safe and pleasant atmosphere. House rules are also important for teaching principles and establishing mutual respect. They inculcate ideals like compassion, honesty, and justice, urging people to respect each other with regard and understanding. To build successful home rules, it's vital to engage all family members in the conversation. This collaborative approach guarantees that everyone's interests and concerns are recognized, establishing a sense of ownership and commitment to obeying the rules.Establishing detailed house rules is a critical step towards a well-organized, courteous, and happy family.

These rules provide a framework for everyday living, enabling family members to cohabit peacefully, acquire fundamental values, and create a pleasant and welcoming atmosphere.

Consistency in discipline

Consistency in discipline is the basis of good parenting, teaching, and personal growth. It requires maintaining a constant attitude toward enforcing rules, expectations, and penalties. This constancy is crucial for various reasons. Firstly, it creates a secure and predictable atmosphere for children and people to develop. When rules are constantly enforced, children learn what is expected of them, leading to a feeling of security and stability. This regularity helps individuals develop self-discipline and responsibility.

Consistency also helps create trust.

When parents or authority figures regularly follow through with incentives and penalties, it promotes confidence and credibility. Individuals realize that acts have consequences, and promises are honored, building a foundation of trust in relationships. Besides, consistency underlines the significance of responsibility. When rules are implemented consistently, people recognize that they are accountable for their behavior. This responsibility supports personal growth and development. In educational contexts, consistency in punishment is vital for sustaining a healthy and respectful classroom culture. It fosters justice since pupils recognize that rules apply equally to everyone, avoiding favoritism or prejudice.

Consistency also assists in creating enduring habits.

Whether it's a youngster learning excellent manners or an adult attempting to break a harmful habit, repeating conduct forms one's character. A consistent approach to discipline promotes these desirable habits and behaviors over time.

Consistency in discipline is the basis of good parenting, teaching, and personal development.

It gives consistency, fosters trust, promotes responsibility, and helps establish enduring habits. By maintaining a consistent approach to enforcing rules and consequences, people may build a supportive and productive atmosphere in which personal growth can thrive.

Teaching responsibility

Teaching responsibility is a crucial part of character development and personal progress. It empowers people with the skills and mentality essential to fulfilling their commitments, both to themselves and to society. The process of establishing responsibility starts at an early age, since parents and educators have a significant role in forming a child's perspective on accountability. Responsibility requires the capacity to make educated choices, accept responsibility for one's actions, and weigh the implications of those acts. It involves several areas, including completing obligations at home, school, work, and in the community. By teaching responsibility, people learn to manage their time effectively, prioritize work, and establish realistic objectives. Moreover, imparting accountability develops ethical conduct and integrity. It encourages people to be honest and dependable, fostering trust in personal and professional relationships. Responsible people are more prepared to face problems, adjust to changing circumstances, and endure hardship. Teaching responsibility goes beyond merely giving information, it requires role modeling, mentoring, and the chance for people to practice and learn from their failures. This process helps people become self-reliant, proactive, and contributing members of society, eventually leading to a more responsible and accountable world.

Chapter 5

Honesty and integrity

Teaching truthfulness

Modeling good behavior

Dealing with lies

Honesty and Integrity

Honesty and integrity are important concepts that support moral behavior and serve as the pillars of a fair and trustworthy society. These two values are intimately interwoven and sometimes used interchangeably, although they have unique features. Honesty comprises sincerity and straightforwardness in communication. It includes the act of presenting facts as they are, without distortion or falsehood. Honesty also goes to being truthful and open in one's actions and intentions. A person who practices honesty is straightforward, open, and dependable, winning the confidence and respect of others. Integrity, on the other hand, goes beyond honesty. It incorporates a deeper feeling of moral uprightness. Someone with integrity not only tells the truth but continuously behaves in accordance with their ideals and values. They are led by a strong moral compass and keep their values even when confronted with hardships or temptations.

Together, honesty and integrity generate a tremendous force for generating confidence and credibility. They are vital in personal interactions, professional situations, and even on a social level.

People who exemplify these values tend to have long-lasting and deep relationships, and they are generally recognized as role models for their persistent dedication to doing what is right. In a society where dishonesty and a lack of integrity may destroy trust and hurt people and communities, appreciating and practicing honesty and integrity is crucial. These values not only enhance our lives with sincerity and trust but also contribute to the advancement of society as a whole.

Teaching truthfulness

Teaching honesty is a fundamental part of character development and ethical education. Truthfulness, which incorporates honesty and sincerity, is a moral virtue that has far-reaching ramifications for personal relationships, professional achievement, and the general well-being of society. Educators and parents have a crucial influence on teaching honesty to young people. They may start by practicing this behavior themselves, since children typically learn by example. Open communication is crucial, allowing youngsters to express themselves honestly and without fear of punishment. It's vital to establish an atmosphere where errors are perceived as chances for progress rather than causes for hiding. Additionally, emphasizing the virtues of empathy and compassion helps young brains realize the need for honesty. Understanding how lying can injure people and weaken trust may be a valuable lesson. Teaching critical thinking and the capacity to assess information may also help people identify truth from deception in a world saturated with disinformation. In educational contexts, the curriculum may contain teachings on ethics, moral issues, and decision-making, all of which can enhance honesty. Encouraging talks about real-life circumstances and their ethical consequences encourages students to engage with the complexity of truth and honesty. Teaching honesty not only provides people with a moral compass but also helps to build a community founded on trust and integrity. It develops responsibility and respect in personal and professional interactions and creates a culture where truth is valued as a basis for growth and wellness.

Modeling good behavior

Modeling good conduct is a crucial component of molding positive character and promoting a healthy society. It includes people, particularly role models, displaying ethical, courteous, and responsible behavior for others to follow. Firstly, modeling appropriate conduct is vital in family contexts. Parents, as major role models, demonstrate traits like compassion, empathy, and honesty, which children absorb and copy. This shapes their values and helps them develop into responsible, empathetic individuals. In educational institutions, instructors play a significant role in modeling proper conduct. Their activities impact pupils' attitudes towards study, respect for classmates, and discipline. A teacher who demonstrates tolerance and respect urges pupils to do the same. Furthermore, companies and organizations gain from leaders who exemplify ethical and professional conduct. Leaders that display honesty, fairness, and responsibility establish a company culture of trust and productivity. Employees are more inclined to adhere to business principles when they perceive their leaders embracing them. In larger cultures, prominent people, celebrities, and influencers hold enormous influence. Their acts may alter society's norms and values. When they model positive conduct, such as environmental responsibility or humanitarian endeavors, they urge their followers to do the same. Modeling good conduct is a multi-faceted process that changes people and society. It originates in the home, expands to educational institutions, impacts business culture, and pervades via the conduct of prominent personalities. It is a tremendous force for creating excellent character and promoting responsible citizenship.

Dealing with lies

Dealing with lying is a complicated and crucial component of human connection. When presented with lies, it's vital to tackle the issue with empathy and compassion. First and foremost, one should analyze the motive behind the lie. Some falsehoods may be innocuous, while others might be harmful. Open communication is crucial to handling lying properly. For white falsehoods or those aimed at shielding sentiments, it's frequently preferable to gently address the matter and emphasize your preference for honesty. In more extreme circumstances, when trust is at issue, a direct talk may be essential to learn the truth and repair trust. It's crucial to avoid a confrontational or accusing tone while dealing with falsehoods, since this might lead to defensiveness. Instead, foster openness, stressing the need for trust in every connection. Moreover, self-reflection is vital; we must understand our own capacity for deceit and the influence of our words on others. In essence, dealing with falsehoods requires a sophisticated and intelligent strategy built on empathy, open communication, and a dedication to honesty and trust.

Chapter 6

Kindness and empathy

Cultivating compassion

Encouraging acts of kindness

Bullying and its consequences

Kindness and empathy

Kindness and empathy are two intimately interwoven attributes that constitute the foundations of compassionate human interactions and a healthy society. They serve as guideposts for moral and ethical behavior, enhancing individual lives and maintaining the fabric of communities. Kindness, at its heart, encompasses actions of compassion, charity, and regard for others. It is the personification of the golden rule: treating people as you would want to be treated. Kind folks go out of their way to aid, encourage, and elevate others around them. This may appear through modest, ordinary acts like a welcoming smile, holding the door open, or delivering words of support. It is a worldwide language that transcends borders and unites individuals on a basic human level. Empathy complements compassion by helping us to comprehend and share the experiences of others. It is the capacity to put oneself in someone else's shoes, to listen and watch with sensitivity, and to react with true care and understanding. Empathy develops strong emotional connections, validating others' feelings and making them feel really seen and cherished.

When kindness and empathy connect, they generate a tremendous force for good development. Kindness generally starts with sympathetic empathy, as we endeavor to know the needs, difficulties, and emotions of others around us. This combination not only enables us to lend a helping hand but also to deliver that aid in ways that authentically address the specific situations of others. In a society frequently defined by conflict and disagreement, kindness and empathy are vital components in bridging gaps, developing inclusion, and establishing a culture of compassion and support. They contribute to personal satisfaction, build interpersonal connections, and promote a more peaceful community where people feel really connected, supported, and understood. Cultivating kindness and empathy is not merely a moral requirement; it is the way to a more empathic, compassionate, and egalitarian society.

Cultivating compassion

Cultivating compassion is a meaningful path that leads to personal development and constructive social transformation. Compassion is the capacity to sympathize with the pain of others and the sincere desire to relieve that suffering. It goes beyond simple pity, since it requires an active commitment to make the world a better place for everyone. To grow compassion, one must first acquire self-awareness and emotional intelligence. This self-awareness helps people comprehend their own emotions and prejudices, helping them to connect more fully to the experiences of others. Compassion is not confined to empathizing with individuals who are similar to us; it extends to all creatures, establishing a feeling of global connectivity. Practicing compassion requires actions of kindness and empathy towards others. Whether it's through volunteering, lending a listening ear, or just being there for someone in need, these activities cultivate compassion inside us. Additionally, mindfulness and meditation may strengthen our capacity to be present and responsive to the pain of others.

Compassion also plays a significant role in tackling social concerns including injustice, bigotry, and poverty.

By fostering compassion, people and communities may work together to achieve good change and advocate for justice and fairness. Cultivating compassion is a transforming path that starts with self-awareness, continues with acts of kindness, and eventually leads to a more compassionate and fair society. This fundamental characteristic enhances our lives and the lives of those we touch, building a world that values empathy and understanding.

Encouraging acts of kindness

Encouraging acts of kindness is a crucial undertaking that builds a more empathetic and peaceful community. Kindness, sometimes defined as the purest form of human contact, has the capacity to produce a ripple effect. To encourage acts of compassion, numerous ways may be implemented. First and foremost, education plays a key role in cultivating compassion. Schools and communities should stress teaching empathy, inclusivity, and the significance of little gestures. By establishing these principles in the younger generation, we assure a future where compassion is a standard rather than an exception. Besides, providing a personal example is vital. When people, especially those in positions of authority, display kindness in their everyday lives, it sends a strong message to others. Acts of generosity may be infectious, prompting individuals to pay them forward. Creating chances for participation and community service also helps promote compassion. By participating in activities that benefit others, people feel the delight of helping, supporting the concept that kindness is its own reward. In addition, social media and technology may be leveraged to promote compassion. Campaigns and challenges that encourage acts of benevolence may become viral, motivating many individuals to engage. Ultimately, fostering acts of kindness is not merely a moral requirement but also a method of establishing better, more connected communities.

By teaching, leading by example, providing service opportunities, and utilizing the power of digital media, we can make kindness a cornerstone of our society, resulting in a more compassionate and sympathetic world.

Bullying and its consequences

Bullying, a common societal scourge, inflicts devastating repercussions on people and society. It appears in numerous ways, such as verbal, physical, or cyberbullying, and frequently starts in infancy, extending throughout adulthood. The ramifications of bullying are far-reaching and dangerous. On a personal level, victims of bullying feel emotional discomfort, worry, sadness, and a lowered sense of self-worth. The trauma may lead to long-term psychological scars that damage one's mental health throughout life. Additionally, victims may turn to harmful coping techniques, such as drug misuse, in an effort to ease their agony. Bullying not only damages the people involved but also creates a poisonous climate inside communities and schools. It generates a culture of dread, destroying trust and empathy. Moreover, it might impair academic and professional growth, leading to diminished productivity and poor social integration. Addressing bullying needs a multi-pronged effort, including schools, parents, and the government. Promoting empathy, tolerance, and respect via anti-bullying initiatives and stringent rules is crucial. Counseling and support services should be in place to help victims recover and abusers learn the implications of their conduct. Bullying's ramifications are vast and negative, hurting people and society as a whole. Eradicating this prevalent problem needs deliberate efforts to build a safe and inclusive workplace for everyone.

Chapter 7

Respect and tolerance

Promoting respect for others

Embracing diversity

Addressing prejudice and discrimination.

Respect and tolerance

Respect and tolerance are two fundamental qualities that govern a healthy and inclusive society, encouraging understanding, unity, and the well-being of people and groups. Respect implies acknowledging the fundamental value and dignity of every individual. It implies respecting people with decency, understanding, and compassion, regardless of their background, beliefs, or viewpoints. Respect extends to accepting personal limits and decisions, understanding the importance of variety, and embracing the distinctive attributes that make each individual special. It establishes a foundation of trust and good esteem in both personal and social interactions. Tolerance complements respect by highlighting the acceptance of differences, especially when they depart from one's own ideas or ideals. Tolerance does not imply agreement but rather the desire to live peacefully with varied viewpoints, cultures, and identities. It encourages a society where people are free to express themselves without fear of discrimination, bias, or exclusion.

When respect and tolerance merge, they build a culture of inclusion and understanding. Respect encourages people to appreciate each other's uniqueness, while tolerance creates an attitude of acceptance, especially in the face of conflicts.

This potent mix helps manage the challenges of a varied and interconnected world with elegance and open-mindedness. In our increasingly globalized and multicultural society, respect and tolerance are crucial to bridging gaps, minimizing tensions, and building social cohesion. They lay the basis for a more fair and equal society, where everyone has a place and a voice. By accepting these ideas, we contribute to a more compassionate and peaceful society where the richness of human variety is valued and every person is treated with the respect and care they deserve. Promoting respect for others is a vital foundation of a healthy and inclusive society. Respect is the cornerstone of healthy human relationships, transcending ethnic, racial, and gender divides. To cultivate this ideal, we must embrace empathy, understanding, and open communication.

Empathy is at the core of respect.

It requires the capacity to put oneself in another person's shoes, respecting their experiences and viewpoints. By exercising empathy, we may better recognize the uniqueness of each person, ultimately developing a culture of respect. Understanding is another crucial factor. When we take the time to learn about varied origins, views, and experiences, we create an atmosphere that appreciates diversity. This understanding lowers preconceptions and biases, leading to more fundamental regard for one another.

Open communication has a vital role in respect-building.

Honest and polite talks help us to confront disputes, clarify misconceptions, and discover common ground. Active listening, in particular, guarantees that every voice is heard and respected. Respect for others should extend beyond words to deeds. Demonstrating respect via compassion, justice, and inclusivity further emphasizes its value. When we respect others, we produce a positive ripple effect that may improve our communities and society as a whole. Promoting respect for others rests on empathy, understanding, and open communication. It's not only a good emotion; it's a crucial basis for developing a more peaceful and inclusive society where every person is recognized and treated with dignity.

Embracing diversity

Embracing diversity is a crucial foundation of a vibrant, inclusive society. It means not simply acknowledging differences in race, ethnicity, gender, religion, or culture, but appreciating and respecting them. In doing so, we build an atmosphere where every person is recognized for their unique viewpoints and experiences. Diversity has a range of advantages. It increases our awareness of the world, increases empathy, and eliminates prejudice. Diverse teams are more inventive since they bring a diverse variety of talents and ideas to the table. Moreover, embracing diversity fosters equitable chances, guaranteeing that no one encounters prejudice based on their background. In a globalized world, embracing diversity is not merely a moral duty but also an economic one. It helps organizations access a larger client base and tap into a greater talent pool. Furthermore, it stimulates cultural interaction, encouraging tolerance and solidarity. Embracing diversity is a constant process involving education, open-mindedness, and the removal of entrenched prejudices. By appreciating and accepting our differences, we can establish a peaceful society that lives on the power of its variety.

Addressing prejudice and discrimination

Addressing prejudice and discrimination is a vital priority for establishing a more inclusive and equal society. Prejudice, entrenched in preconceived conceptions and prejudices, frequently leads to discrimination, resulting in systematic injustices and unfair treatment of people or groups based on their color, ethnicity, gender, religion, or other traits. To counteract prejudice and discrimination, education plays a key role. Promoting diversity and inclusion in schools and workplaces is crucial. Teaching about diverse cultures, histories, and views helps break down preconceptions and builds empathy. It's also crucial to foster open discussions on difficult matters, enabling individuals to share their experiences and better understand one another.

Legislation and policy are significant weapons for combating prejudice.

Laws that safeguard the rights of disadvantaged groups and promote equal opportunity are vital. However, it's also necessary to enforce these rules aggressively, holding those who discriminate responsible for their acts.

Media and popular culture are significant in creating cultural standards.

They may either perpetuate preconceptions or question them. Encouraging media sources to offer a more varied and nuanced image of society may have a tremendous influence on popular opinions. Individuals have a personal duty to overcome their biases and prejudices.

Self-reflection and actively seeking out other opinions might help individuals become more inclusive and sympathetic. Engaging in friendship and assisting disadvantaged populations may also have a huge effect. Addressing discrimination and prejudice is a complicated process that involves a joint effort from people, communities, organizations, and governments. Through education, law, media, and personal development, we may strive towards a more fair and equitable society where everyone is treated with dignity and respect.

Chapter 8

Responsibility and accountability

Chores and responsibilities

Handling mistakes and consequences

Preparing for independence.

Responsibility and accountability

Responsibility and accountability are two key foundations that promote ethical conduct and successful functioning, both in the personal and corporate realms. Responsibility is the acknowledgement of one's commitments and the understanding of the repercussions of one's actions. It entails a serious commitment to executing tasks and accepting responsibility for decisions. Embracing responsibility is a characteristic of proactivity since it motivates people to actively participate in problem-solving and make positive contributions to their communities and organizations.

Accountability goes hand in hand with responsibility by having people account for their actions. It involves clear communication and the documentation of assignments and decisions. When people are responsible, openness is fostered and trust is developed, which is particularly crucial in team dynamics and organizational settings. It guarantees that individuals are liable for their duties, which develops dependability and increases efficiency. Together, responsibility and accountability establish a culture of honesty, trust, and efficiency.

Individuals who apply these concepts to their lives are more likely to fulfill deadlines, generate high-quality work, and build excellent working relationships. In organizations, these values inspire cooperation, mutual support, and a dedication to common objectives. In essence, responsibility and accountability are crucial traits that lead to ethical conduct and good results. They stimulate personal development, create trust among people, and contribute to the general benefit of society.

Chores and responsibilities

Chores and responsibilities serve a critical role in molding our everyday lives, nurturing fundamental life skills, and preserving peaceful homes and communities. Chores, generally linked with ordinary activities like cleaning, cooking, and washing, are more than monotonous responsibilities; they develop discipline, time management, and a feeling of responsibility. From an early age, children may learn responsibility by helping with home duties. This not only lessens the strain on parents but also teaches youngsters about responsibility, cooperation, and the importance of hard work. These early teachings lay the groundwork for their future duties as responsible adults. In a larger context, obligations extend beyond home activities. In the workplace, people are responsible for particular jobs and duties that contribute to the overall performance of the firm. Moreover, in society, people have civic obligations, including observing laws, paying taxes, and participating in the democratic process by voting. Balancing duties and obligations is crucial to maintaining good work-life harmony. It demands efficient time management and the capacity to prioritize things. When duties are handled evenly within a home, it encourages collaboration and decreases stress for all members. Chores and obligations are the pillars of personal development and community harmony. They function as a crucible for imparting values, molding character, and developing a sense of purpose. By recognizing the value of these everyday tasks, we may cultivate responsible people who contribute effectively to their families, businesses, and communities.

Handling shortcomings and their repercussions

Handling shortcomings and their repercussions is a crucial skill for personal and professional progress. When faced with mistakes, the first step is to admit them. Denial just exacerbates the situation and precludes effective learning. Taking responsibility for one's errors is a sign of maturity and accountability. Once a mistake is detected, it's vital to evaluate its reasons. Understanding why the mistake happened helps in avoiding its recurrence. This process includes self-reflection and, where appropriate, receiving criticism from others. Mistakes are excellent chances for development since they show areas for improvement. Consequences might range from slight inconveniences to serious setbacks. To handle these repercussions, it's vital to design a plan of action. This may entail fixing the error, making reparations, or reducing the consequences. Communicating openly and honestly with individuals impacted is crucial, as it creates confidence and displays a willingness to solve the problem Furthermore, resilience is crucial in addressing oversights. It's crucial to remember that everyone makes mistakes, and they do not determine one's value or ability. Learning from errors and utilizing them as stepping stones to development is a characteristic of a resilient person. Handling shortcomings and their repercussions includes acknowledgment, analysis, action, and resilience. It is through this process that we not only fix faults but also develop as people, increasing our talents and character. Preparing for independence is a complicated process that people, communities, and countries undertake to attain self-sufficiency and autonomy. It involves several components, including financial, emotional, and practical preparations, to facilitate a seamless transition from dependence to self-reliance.

Below are the factors that contribute to a comprehensive strategy for preparing for independence.

Financial independence

Achieving financial stability is a vital component of preparing for independence. This entails managing personal money, saving, investing, and lowering debt. Individuals must develop a budget, construct an emergency fund, and make sensible financial choices to safeguard their economic future.

Education and skill development Education and skill acquisition are vital for personal and professional freedom. Gaining knowledge and competence in one's chosen sector helps people pursue their career ambitions and contribute effectively to society. Lifelong learning is necessary to be competitive in an ever-evolving environment.

Emotional and mental resilience

Preparing for independence also requires establishing emotional and mental resilience. This involves growing self-confidence, managing stress, and establishing a positive mentality. Strong mental health is vital for conquering problems and making wise choices.

Social and community connections

Interpersonal ties and community participation play a significant role in preparing for independence. A robust support network may provide essential advice, help, and emotional support during times of transition or uncertainty. Community engagement develops a sense of belonging and shared responsibility.

Legal and civic awareness

Understanding the legal and civic obligations is vital for gaining independence. This entails an understanding of one's rights and duties as an activist, as well as active involvement in civic activities, like voting, to influence the future of one's community and country.

Goal setting and planning

Setting clear objectives and having a well-structured plan are key milestones on the route to independence. Individuals and groups must identify their goals and detail the required measures to attain them. Regularly examining and updating these strategies ensures they stay relevant.

Health and well-being

Physical and mental health are crucial for independence. Adopting a healthy lifestyle, keeping a balanced diet, and obtaining medical treatment when required are key parts of guaranteeing well-being. Healthy people are better suited to manage obstacles and strive for independence.

Sustainability and environment

Environmental concern is increasingly interwoven with the notion of independence. Preparing for independence involves being cognizant of sustainability, lowering one's environmental imprint, and safeguarding natural resources to preserve a healthy world for future generations.

Chapter 9

Resilience and problem-solving

Teaching coping skills

Encouraging perseverance

Navigating tough times

Resilience and problem-solving

Resilience and problem-solving are two interconnected skills that equip people to face life's obstacles and uncertainties with grace and efficacy. Resilience is the capacity to bounce back from adversity, adapt to changing circumstances, and sustain emotional and mental well-being. It requires a mix of inner strength, emotional intelligence, and coping techniques. Resilient people not only withstand adversities but frequently emerge from them stronger, equipped with great life lessons. This trait helps people endure setbacks, stress, and even failure with a good attitude, eventually leading to personal growth and development. Problem-solving, on the other hand, is the talent of finding answers to difficult or daily situations. It needs critical thinking, inventiveness, and flexibility. Problem solvers address issues with an open mind and a willingness to develop and execute effective solutions. They welcome hurdles as chances for development and creativity, ultimately contributing positively to their personal and professional lives.

The link between resilience and problem-solving is synergistic. Resilience empowers people with the mental and emotional strength to handle challenges without succumbing to stress, whereas problem-solving develops resilience by improving one's ability to adapt and overcome.

Together, they constitute a potent mix that empowers people to succeed in an ever-changing environment, making them great assets in both personal and professional domains.

Teaching coping skills

Teaching coping skills is a critical component of human growth and mental well-being. Coping skills are the tactics and procedures people use to handle stress, emotions, and tough circumstances successfully. These talents help individuals manage life's problems with perseverance and emotional equilibrium.

First and foremost, teaching coping skills empowers people with the capacity to detect their emotions and pressures. This self-awareness is the basis upon which successful coping is constructed. It allows individuals to recognize when they are feeling overwhelmed, nervous, or disturbed, which is the first step in finding appropriate strategies to manage these emotions. Furthermore, teaching coping skills involves a broad variety of strategies. These include mindfulness meditation, deep breathing exercises, and cognitive reframing, which help people manage stress and anxiety. Additionally, problem-solving skills and seeking social support are crucial coping techniques for handling life's obstacles. Teaching coping skills is particularly vital in educational contexts since it helps students handle academic stress and peer interactions. It builds emotional intelligence and resilience, eventually increasing academic achievement and general mental health. In the workplace, training in coping skills is also important. It increases employee well-being by lowering absenteeism and enhancing productivity. Coping skills assist people to manage work-related stress and maintain a good work-life balance. Teaching coping skills is a crucial life skill that improves emotional well-being and stress management. These talents allow people to tackle life's obstacles with resilience, giving them the tools they need to lead happier, more productive lives.

Encouraging perseverance

Encouraging persistence is a crucial component of personal and professional progress. Perseverance, typically described as the constant pursuit of a goal despite hurdles or failures, is a trait that differentiates people who realize their aspirations from those who quit them early. To foster endurance, it is vital to provide a supportive atmosphere. This may be done through positive reinforcement and acknowledgement of efforts, even when the effects are not immediate or evident. Celebrating modest achievements throughout the path helps improve motivation and keep a positive mindset. Moreover, delivering constructive comments helps people learn from their experiences and become more resilient in the face of adversity. Setting reasonable and achievable objectives is another significant component. Unattainable aims may lead to dissatisfaction and demotivation, whereas achievable goals enable people to measure progress and keep a sense of purpose. Encouraging folks to divide their overall objectives into smaller, doable tasks might make the route to accomplishment less overwhelming. Influence models have a crucial impact on developing persistence. Sharing examples of people who have overcome hurdles and failures on their route to achievement may encourage and comfort others experiencing problems. Learning from others' experiences helps foster the sense that obstacles are not insurmountable but rather possibilities for progress. Fostering a growth mentality, where problems are regarded as chances to learn and improve, is crucial to fostering endurance. Embracing failures as stepping stones toward achievement may convert setbacks into important learning. Encouraging persistence entails establishing a supportive atmosphere, setting reasonable objectives, offering constructive criticism, and developing a development mentality. By doing so, people are more likely to continue in their endeavors, eventually reaching their objectives and completing their potential.

Navigating tough times

Dealing with peer pressure is an essential component of teenage and even adult life. It refers to the effect that peers may have on an individual's decisions, actions, and beliefs. While peer pressure may occasionally lead to beneficial consequences, such as stimulating personal development or cultivating healthy behaviors, it frequently offers obstacles. One successful method for overcoming peer pressure is building strong self-esteem and a sense of identity. When people have a firm knowledge of their values and ideas, they are more able to withstand negative peer pressure that may contradict their principles. Open and honest communication with friends and family also plays a critical part in addressing peer pressure. Trusted confidants may give support, advice, and varied viewpoints, helping people make educated choices. Additionally, establishing limits and saying "no" when appropriate is a crucial ability to express one's individuality. Building a network of friends who share similar beliefs and objectives may help decrease the harmful influence of peer pressure. Surrounding oneself with good influences may create a supportive atmosphere that supports personal development and resilience. Addressing peer pressure is a key life skill. By growing self-esteem, promoting open communication, establishing boundaries, and cultivating a supportive peer group, people may successfully traverse the complicated terrain of peer influence and make choices that accord with their actual selves.

Chapter 10

Self-esteem and confidence

Fostering positive self-Image

Encouraging self-expression

Dealing with peer pressure

Self-esteem and confidence

Self-esteem and confidence are vital components of one's emotional well-being. Self-esteem refers to the general view one has of oneself, incorporating sentiments of self-worth and self-respect. It's influenced by events, relationships, and self-perception. Confidence, on the other hand, is the conviction in one's talents and the bravery to act upon them. Healthy self-esteem is the cornerstone of a confident person. When one has a good self-image, they are more inclined to approach obstacles with optimism and resilience. Confidence, in turn, is the outward manifestation of this self-assurance. It entails trusting one's judgment and talents, leading to boldness and the ability to pursue personal and professional objectives. Nurturing self-esteem and confidence entails self-acceptance, self-compassion, and recognizing personal strengths. Constructive self-talk, creating and attaining modest objectives, and seeking assistance when required are crucial tactics. Critically, learning from setbacks and disappointments may increase confidence in the long term. Self-esteem and confidence are interdependent and crucial traits for personal development and enjoyment. Cultivating them involves self-awareness, effort, and a supportive environment, eventually leading to a more pleasant and successful existence.

Fostering positive self-image

Fostering a healthy self-image is vital for one's mental and emotional well-being. It covers the growth of self-esteem, self-worth, and self-acceptance. Building a good self-image starts with self-awareness, knowing one's strengths and flaws, and admitting that faults are a part of being human. Self-compassion is a vital component of this path. Treating oneself with love and forgiveness enhances resilience and mental stability. Positive self-talk plays a key function, as our internal conversation may either strengthen or degrade our self-image. Social support is crucial to fostering self-esteem. Surrounding oneself with encouraging and affirming people promotes a feeling of belonging and affirmation. Additionally, defining and attaining personal objectives may enhance confidence and self-worth. Fostering a healthy self-image is a continuous process that includes self-awareness, self-compassion, positive self-talk, and a supportive social network. A strong and good self-image not only increases individual well-being but also helps with better relationships and personal progress.

Encouraging self-expression

Encouraging self-expression is an important part of human growth and society's progress. It encourages people to voice their ideas, emotions, and creativity, creating a more inclusive and understanding environment. Self-expression takes different forms, from creative efforts like painting, music, and writing to verbal communication and body language. By supporting self-expression, we unleash the potential for innovation and creativity. When individuals are empowered to express themselves freely, they might think outside the box and come up with novel ideas. It's through self-expression that artists produce timeless masterpieces, scientists make new discoveries, and social change is launched. Besides, self-expression has a key role in mental and emotional well-being. It assists people to release pent-up emotions, relieve tension, and improve self-confidence.

In a society where mental health is a rising problem, fostering self-expression may be a therapeutic outlet. In the framework of society, embracing self-expression encourages tolerance and understanding. It helps us to respect other viewpoints, cultures, and backgrounds, creating empathy and eliminating prejudice. In essence, a culture that encourages self-expression is one that supports a more caring and peaceful environment. Encouraging self-expression is a strong stimulus for personal and social growth. It develops creativity, helps mental health, and promotes a more open and understanding environment. Since we go ahead, let's continue to enable everyone to express themselves genuinely and without fear, since it is through their unique voices that we can build a brighter future for all.

Dealing with peer pressure

Dealing with peer pressure may be a challenging but vital component of a person's life, especially throughout adolescence and early adulthood. It refers to the impact that friends and acquaintances have on an individual's choices, conduct, and attitudes. While peer pressure may occasionally lead to favorable consequences, such as motivating one to achieve or adopt healthy behaviors, it frequently offers obstacles. To manage peer pressure successfully, it's vital to build self-awareness and confidence. Understanding one's values, priorities, and aspirations may give a solid basis for rejecting unwanted influences. An open conversation with trustworthy adults or mentors may also provide helpful assistance. Furthermore, creating a supportive network of friends who share similar beliefs may help buffer the effects of damaging social pressure. Learning to say no assertively and making educated choices are key skills. It's vital to remember that being independent and loyal to oneself is a sign of strength, and fighting negative social pressure may lead to personal development, self-respect, and a better future.

Chapter 11

Talents and passions

Identifying interests

Encouraging hobbies and skills

Balancing academic and extracurricular activities

Talents and passions

Talents and passions are the driving factors behind our personality and purpose in life. Talents are intrinsic skills and abilities that humans possess, influencing a wide range of abilities, from pleasing talents such as painting and music to analytical skills like problem-solving or calculation. These qualities frequently serve as the building blocks for our endeavors and areas of competence. Passions, on the other hand, are the deep interests and emotional connections we have with certain activities, causes, or issues. They feed our drive, give direction, and maintain our excitement throughout our trip. When our abilities match with our interests, we find our genuine callings; when work feels like pleasure, commitment becomes a labor of love. The convergence of abilities and interests may lead to outstanding results and a feeling of contentment. It empowers people to thrive in their chosen pathways, whether it's in professional employment, artistic efforts, or personal hobbies. Moreover, the confluence of abilities and interests stimulates creativity, innovation, and personal progress, leading to a life full of purpose and joy. This interaction between our intrinsic skills and our innermost interests provides a strong sense of purpose, propelling us to attain our greatest potential and contribute to the world in a unique and meaningful manner.

Identifying interests

Identity interest is a complicated and diverse notion that plays a key part in developing an individual's self-image and social relationships. It refers to the dynamic interaction between an individual's changing sense of self and the numerous organizations or communities to which they belong. These groupings may cover features such as race, gender, sexual orientation, religion, culture, and more. Identity interest is the detailed examination of how these components affect one's identity and, in turn, how they affect an individual's interests and passions. This notion is crucial since it dramatically influences human growth and social dynamics. It empowers people to realize who they are, encouraging self-acceptance and honesty. Moreover, it encourages individuals to participate in causes, activities, or affiliations that correspond with their self-identifications, resulting in a feeling of purpose and satisfaction. Identity interest also overlaps with the larger social setting. In a varied and interconnected society, recognizing and honoring identification interests is crucial for encouraging inclusion and understanding. It emphasizes the celebration of diversity and the appreciation of the various viewpoints each individual brings to the table. Embracing these differences may lead to increased empathy and cooperation among people and communities. dentity interest is a basic feature of human life. It helps people better grasp themselves and their role in society, promoting self-realization and meaningful social ties. By understanding and embracing the complex nature of identity interest, we may build a more inclusive and peaceful environment where individuals can be their real selves while enjoying the richness of variety.

Encouraging hobbies and skills

Encouraging interests and abilities is vital for personal growth and general well-being. Hobbies give people a chance to decompress, destress, and find delight in their free time. They give an opportunity for creativity, self-expression, and a vacation from the stresses of regular life. Engaging in a pastime may enhance self-esteem and create a feeling of achievement, whether it's through painting, playing a musical instrument, gardening, or any other love. Hobbies frequently turn into useful abilities. For example, someone enthusiastic about photography may ultimately grow into a good photographer, opening possibilities for a prospective profession. Encouraging these interests from an early age may lead to the discovery of lifetime passions and even future careers.In the context of children and schooling, cultivating interests and skills is equally crucial. It fosters well-rounded growth, helping youngsters find their interests and abilities. Encouraging hobbies encourages discipline, patience, and resilience as people try to better their talents. It also boosts cognitive ability and problem-solving, since individuals frequently need to think creatively to thrive in their chosen hobbies. Encouraging hobbies and talents is an investment in personal development and pleasure. It encourages self-discovery, cultivates abilities, and gives a constructive outlet for stress release. It is a portal to a more meaningful and fuller existence, allowing people to develop their potential to the utmost.

Balancing academic and extracurricular activities

Balancing academic and extracurricular activities is vital for a well-rounded and effective school experience. Students must achieve harmony between their education and the different extracurricular hobbies accessible to them. This balance not only supports personal development but also boosts future opportunities. Academics serve as the cornerstone of a student's educational path. A solid academic performance is vital for gaining scholarships, college admissions, and potential professional prospects. Therefore, students should prioritize their academics and construct efficient study plans. Simultaneously, partaking in extracurricular activities benefits students' lives.

These activities, whether they entail sports, clubs, or volunteering, give possibilities for personal growth, leadership, and sociability. Extracurriculars give a platform to pursue hobbies, discover new interests, and acquire key skills like collaboration and time management. To properly balance both, students must develop time management skills. Prioritizing work, creating objectives, and keeping a disciplined routine are crucial. Moreover, open communication with instructors and extracurricular leaders may help build a supportive atmosphere for balancing both responsibilities. Balancing scholastic and extracurricular activities is an important ability that prepares pupils for the rigors of life. It cultivates a comprehensive approach to personal development and guarantees that students not only thrive academically but also acquire the social and life skills essential to living in the future.

Chapter 12

Values and beliefs

Encouraging critical thinking

Discussing religion and spirituality

Exploring ethical challenges

Values and beliefs

Values and beliefs are essential components of human identity and culture, impacting our choices, behaviors, and interactions with the environment. Values are the concepts and criteria by which people and communities determine what is right and wrong, influencing ethical decisions and priorities. These beliefs are frequently firmly imprinted from early infancy and represent cultural, moral, and personal attitudes. Beliefs, on the other hand, are the beliefs and convictions we have about the nature of reality, the world, and our role within it. They may cover religious, spiritual, philosophical, and even scientific views. Beliefs serve as cognitive frameworks that shape our perceptions, attitudes, and interpretations of the world around us. The connection between values and beliefs is deep and significant. Our values may be informed by our beliefs, as well as impact the creation of our beliefs. They collectively form our moral compass and ethical code, impacting our interactions with others and the choices we make in numerous facets of life, including relationships, employment, and social involvement. Values and beliefs also play a key role in cultural variety, contributing to the diverse fabric of human communities. They offer the ethical and moral framework for societies, defining norms, laws, and social contracts.

Moreover, the ongoing examination and reevaluation of our values and beliefs contribute to personal development, self-discovery, and the evolution of civilizations as they adapt to changing circumstances and ideologies.

Encouraging critical thinking

Encouraging critical thinking is crucial to encouraging intellectual development and problem-solving abilities. It is the practice of actively and critically assessing information, ideas, circumstances, or issues rather than passively taking them at face value. This talent empowers people with the capacity to make reasoned judgments, assess evidence, and think logically. To foster critical thinking, educators and parents play a key role. In schools, it is vital to integrate multidisciplinary and open-ended activities that encourage pupils to think beyond rote memorization. Encouraging inquiries and encouraging dialogues cultivates a culture of inquiry and intellectual discovery. Moreover, exposure to varied viewpoints and ideas is crucial. It broadens one's horizons and helps them to rethink their views and preconceptions. Engaging in debates and conversations, whether in classrooms or daily life, sharpens critical thinking abilities by forcing the analysis of diverse opinions. Real-world applications are also crucial to refining critical thinking. Solving challenging issues or engaging in collaborative initiatives encourages people to employ their cognitive talents. Technology may be a great aid in this process, enabling access to large knowledge resources that necessitate judgment. Ultimately, the growth of critical thinking leads to improved decision-making and problem-solving. It improves creativity, self-reflection, and the capacity to communicate effectively. Encouraging critical thinking is not just a method of training people to manage an increasingly complicated environment but also a crucial ingredient in the recipe for personal and social improvement. Religion and spirituality are complicated and intensely personal parts of human existence, frequently linked but separate in their core. Religion often refers to organized systems of ideas and activities, sometimes institutionalized with a particular code of behavior, doctrines, and rituals.

It serves as an organized framework that links humans to the divine, develops community, and gives moral direction. Spirituality, on the other hand, is more flexible and individualized. It includes an inward journey to discover meaning, purpose, and a connection to something bigger than oneself, typically beyond conventional religious constraints.

Discussing religion and spirituality Discussions on religion and spirituality span a broad variety of ideas and experiences. They may provoke both togetherness and conflict. On one side, religion may draw people together, establishing a sense of belonging and shared ideals. On the other hand, it has been a cause of strife throughout history. Spirituality, in its multiplicity, may be a source of great personal development and a bridge to understanding those with varied ideas. In today's worldwide society, debates about religion and spirituality are more crucial than ever. It's crucial to approach these debates with respect, open-mindedness, and a desire to learn from other views. Such talks may develop tolerance, empathy, and a greater understanding of the many ways in which people seek meaning and connection in their lives.

Exploring ethical challenges

Exploring ethical problems is a vital exercise in comprehending the complicated moral terrain of human choices and behaviors. Ethical difficulties are circumstances when humans are presented with options that test their moral ideals, frequently compelling them to consider contradictory principles. In such instances, people must examine the possible ramifications of their actions for multiple stakeholders and their larger social implications. The study of ethical problems dives into philosophical frameworks including utilitarianism, deontology, virtue ethics, and more, offering a thorough grasp of numerous approaches to ethical decision-making. Furthermore, analyzing ethical challenges fosters critical thinking, empathy, and moral reasoning. It requires humans to manage the complicated balance between opposing ideals such as justice, autonomy, beneficence, and non-maleficence.

These inquiries are vital not just for personal growth but also in professional situations. Ethical challenges are widespread in professions including healthcare, business, law, and technology, requiring ethical skills and a commitment to moral ideals. Ultimately, the exploration of ethical issues helps to create a more conscientious and compassionate society where people are more able to make morally sound decisions, supporting the well-being of everyone and sustaining moral principles in a complicated environment.

Chapter 13

Creating meaningful moment

Strengthening the parent-child relationship

Creating meaningful moment

Creating significant moments is the art of adding depth and importance to our lives. These experiences transcend the everyday, leaving permanent marks on our minds and emotions. They serve as the cornerstone of human connection, personal progress, and emotional well-being. Meaningful moments frequently develop from actual human encounters. A sincere chat with a friend, a warm hug with a loved one, or a shared chuckle with coworkers may convert everyday encounters into treasured memories. They remind us of the beauty in the ordinary. Nature also plays a key part in shaping these moments. A sunset painting the sky with shades of gold, a calm stroll in the woods, or the captivating sound of breaking waves may take us to a world of wonder and tranquility. Such experiences with the natural world inspire a feeling of amazement that lives in our spirits. Furthermore, personal hobbies, like following a passion or helping, may provide deep moments of satisfaction. These events connect with our inner selves, giving us a sense of purpose and success. In a society packed with distractions, stopping to relish significant moments improves our lives and links us to the core of what it means to be human. These moments, whether great or tiny, are the building blocks of a more fulfilled life.

Strengthening the parent-child relationship

Strengthening the parent-child bond is a critical component of good family dynamics. A close link between parents and their children develops emotional well-being, resilience, and general happiness. To do this, communication is important. Open and honest talks create an atmosphere where children feel heard and understood. Quality time spent together is another crucial factor. Engaging in activities that both parents and children love, such as playing games, reading, or just chatting, creates trust and rapport. Additionally, active listening helps parents better appreciate their children's wants and worries. Setting limits with compassion and consistency is vital. Children need structure and discipline to feel safe and secure. Parents who set clear instructions and penalties exhibit their dedication to their child's growth. Besides, showing love is vital. Hugs, words of praise, and acts of love build the emotional connection between parent and child. Celebrating successes, no matter how minor, enhances a child's self-esteem and deepens their link with their parents. Strengthening the parent-child bond depends on open communication, quality time, limits, love, and positive reinforcement. This strategy provides a caring and supportive atmosphere, developing the child's emotional well-being and eventually leading to a happier and healthier family.

Chapter 14

Handling challenges and conflict

Peer influences and friendships

Addressing technology and screen time

Handling challenges and conflict

Handling problems and disagreements is a vital ability for personal and professional progress. It involves a mix of effective communication, emotional intelligence, and problem-solving ability. When presented with problems or disputes, individuals and teams may apply numerous ways to handle these circumstances effectively. First and foremost, active and compassionate communication is vital. Open and honest discussion may help expose the fundamental reasons for disputes and obstacles, promoting a shared understanding of the issues at hand. Listening carefully and understanding the viewpoints of all people involved is vital. Emotional intelligence plays a key role in addressing conflict. Recognizing and controlling one's own emotions while being attentive to the feelings of others might help prevent confrontations from growing. It also helps people respond more carefully rather than reactively. Effective problem-solving is another key component. Identifying the main challenges and providing innovative solutions might lead to resolution. Collaborative problem-solving, when all parties work together to identify common ground, frequently provides the best durable outcomes. Furthermore, it's crucial to be adaptive and flexible while coping with obstacles. Sometimes, the original method may require change when additional facts or viewpoints emerge.

In both personal and professional contexts, good conflict and challenge resolution may enrich relationships, produce a more productive workplace, and encourage personal development. It's a talent that, when learned, allows people and teams to convert challenges into opportunities, eventually contributing to their total success and well-being.

Peer influences and friendships

Peer influences and friendships have a key role in defining an individual's life, especially during the formative years. Friends are not merely companions but also influences who affect one's views, attitudes, and actions. These effects may be both good and detrimental. Positive friendships may provide emotional support, stimulate personal development, and increase self-esteem. They create a feeling of belonging and may motivate people to attain their objectives. In contrast, negative peer effects may lead to dangerous actions, compliance, and even the destruction of personal values. To negotiate this terrain, it's vital to select allies intelligently. Surrounding oneself with individuals who have similar beliefs and objectives may produce a healthy and caring atmosphere. Effective communication, empathy, and dispute resolution are also key abilities for sustaining strong friendships.

Addressing technology and screen time In today's digital world, tackling technology and screen time has become a critical problem. While technology has revolutionized communication, education, and entertainment, excessive screen time may lead to many physical, emotional, and societal difficulties. To achieve a balance, it is vital for people, particularly youngsters, to regulate their screen time wisely. Parents and guardians have a key role in establishing appropriate limits and acting as role models. Encouraging outdoor activities, family connections, and restricting screen usage around mealtimes might help youngsters establish a more balanced relationship with technology. Moreover, educational institutions should incorporate digital literacy and ethical technology usage into their curricula.

Teaching children how to critically examine online information, exercise digital etiquette, and regulate their screen time will empower them to make educated decisions. Beyond the familial and educational arenas, technology corporations also hold a huge duty. They should create platforms and apps with user well-being in mind, adding features that encourage responsible use. Screen time monitoring, digital well-being tools, and app limitations are examples of how technology may aid consumers in regulating their online presence. Individuals themselves must build self-awareness and discipline. They may benefit from tactics such as digital detoxes, putting time limitations on their gadgets, and adopting mindfulness practices to minimize the temptation of endless scrolling. Addressing technology and screen time is a complicated process that requires collaborative initiatives from families, schools, and technology providers, as well as personal responsibility. Striking a good balance between the benefits of technology and a healthy, offline existence is vital for the well-being of people and society as a whole.

Chapter 15

Preparing for the teen years

Discussing puberty and changes

Guiding toward adolescence

Setting the stage for responsible independence

Preparing for the teen years

Preparing for the adolescent years is a vital era in the lives of both youngsters and their parents. Adolescence, which generally extends from ages 13 to 19, is characterized by profound physical, emotional, and cognitive changes. It's a moment of change that demands serious study and planning. For parents, recognizing the developmental changes their child is facing is crucial. Teenagers frequently seek greater freedom, push boundaries, and start on a path to self-discovery. Effective parenting in this era entails striking a balance between allowing liberty and retaining direction and communication. Being personable and providing an atmosphere where kids feel secure enough to express themselves is vital. Open and honest discussion may help create trust and manage the various problems teens may experience, such as peer pressure, academic stress, and identity construction. Teenagers themselves have a vital role in preparing for this time. Developing emotional intelligence, resilience, and decision-making abilities is vital. They must learn to manage the intricacies of peer interactions, make appropriate decisions, and deal with the emotional issues that come throughout adolescence. Education and awareness are crucial for both parents and teens.

Learning about concerns such as puberty, mental health, and drug addiction empowers kids with information to make educated choices. Encouraging teens to participate in extracurricular activities, pursue hobbies, and explore their interests may help them find their passions and improve self-esteem. In essence, preparing for the teen years includes a twofold effort: parents altering their parenting technique and teens learning crucial life skills and self-awareness. Through open communication and support, both parents and teenagers may negotiate this transitional era with more knowledge and confidence.

Discussing puberty and changes

Puberty is a critical period in human development, characterized by a number of physiological and psychological changes. Typically occurring between the ages of 8 and 13 in girls and 9 and 14 in men, puberty is defined by the activation of the endocrine system, resulting in a cascade of alterations. One of the most noticeable physical changes throughout puberty is the development of secondary sexual features. In females, this involves breast growth, the commencement of menstruation, and the widening of the hips. In males, it entails the development of facial hair, the deepening of the voice, and the expansion of the testes. These changes are mostly controlled by hormones like estrogen in females and testosterone in men. Beyond the physical transformations, puberty also brings about substantial psychological changes. Adolescents typically experience an outpouring of emotions, mood swings, and the formation of self-identity. It is a period when peer interactions become more essential and people begin to explore their sexuality. The timing of puberty might vary across people owing to genetic and environmental variables. Early or late puberty may have emotional and social effects, stressing the significance of knowledge and support from parents, guardians, and educated. Puberty is a normal and complicated process, comprising both physical and emotional changes as people move from infancy to maturity. While it may be a stressful period for many, it is crucial to equip teenagers with the knowledge and support they need to manage these changes effectively. Acknowledging the individuality of each individual's path through puberty is vital to ensuring a healthy transition into adulthood.

Guiding toward adolescence

Adolescence is a significant transitional time in a person's life, characterized by physical, emotional, and cognitive changes. Guiding people through this stormy time is vital to encouraging their growth and well-being. Adolescents typically battle with identity development, peer pressure, scholastic problems, and emotional upheaval. Hence, competent mentoring plays a key role in their path. Comprehensive advice covers different areas.

Firstly, it entails open communication. Parents, educators, and mentors must maintain open, non-judgmental channels of communication to enable teenagers to communicate their views and concerns. Active listening and empathy are crucial components of this process. Secondly, teenagers require chances for inquiry and self-discovery. Encouraging children to explore their interests, hobbies, and abilities may benefit identity formation. Providing access to varied extracurricular activities and experiences is vital. Imparting life skills is crucial. Adolescents should be prepared with problem-solving, decision-making, and stress-management abilities. This prepares them for the problems that come their way. Lastly, providing a supportive and loving atmosphere is crucial. Adolescents flourish when they feel protected and appreciated. Building self-esteem and resilience is a continual process that needs a strong support system. Guiding teenagers on their path towards maturity entails open communication, chances for self-discovery, life skill development, and the establishment of a supportive atmosphere. When tackled completely, mentoring throughout this vital time provides the basis for well-adjusted, confident, and resilient people ready to confront the complexity of adulthood.

Setting the stage for responsible independence

Setting the scene for responsible independence is a significant and transforming journey that is necessary for personal growth and social progress. Responsible independence involves not just having the freedom to make decisions but also enduring the repercussions of such actions while considering the welfare of others.

At a personal level, responsible independence starts with self-reliance and self-sufficiency. It entails developing the skills and information required to manage life's obstacles and opportunities. This may comprise financial knowledge, emotional resilience, and a strong work ethic. It allows people to make educated choices and take charge of their lives. From a larger perspective, responsible independence plays a key role in society. It involves being an involved and responsible citizen who contributes positively to the community. Responsible citizens not only engage in civic activities but also consider the influence of their actions on the environment, the economy, and the well-being of others. Education and mentoring are crucial in establishing the scene for responsible independence. Schools, families, and communities should provide direction and support in developing the skills and values required for people to be both independent and responsible. Responsible freedom is the cornerstone of personal progress and social advancement. It is a delicate balance between individual freedom and social obligation. Setting the scene for responsible independence involves an investment in education, mentoring, and the fostering of responsible, self-reliant people who can contribute to a thriving and peaceful community.

Conclusion

In the pages of "Raising Good Tweens of Value," Charles T. Ellison has presented us with a vital direction for steering our tweens towards a destiny of compassion, integrity, and purpose. As we approach the conclusion of this fascinating trip, we find ourselves equipped with important information and practical wisdom. Ellison's comments have paved the way for parenting adolescents who grasp the genuine worth of compassion, respect, and the significance of giving to their communities.

The author's real love for raising the next generation shows through in every chapter. He reminds us that the tween years are essential in developing the character of our children, and he gives real tactics for imparting the principles that will serve them well in adulthood. "Raising Good Tweens of Value" isn't simply a book; it's a handbook for parents and caregivers aiming to build a better world through their children.

May the values acquired here be an essential component for developing a generation of tweens who are not only decent people but also important contributors to society. Happy reading, and much happy parenting.